JAZZGUITAR

DOMINANTCHORDSUBSTITUTIONS

Arpeggio Soloing Vocabulary for The Most Important Chord in Jazz

TIMPETTINGALE

FUNDAMENTALCHANGES

Jazz Guitar Dominant Chord Substitutions

Arpeggio Soloing Vocabulary for The Most Important Chord in Jazz

ISBN: 978-1-78933-406-7

Published by **www.fundamental-changes.com**

www.fundamental-changes.com

Over 12,000 fans on Facebook: **FundamentalChangesInGuitar**

Instagram: **FundamentalChanges**

For over 350 Free Guitar Lessons with Videos Check Out

www.fundamental-changes.com

Cover Image Copyright: Patrick James Eggle Guitars, used by permission

All the audio for this book was recorded with a Patrick James Eggle "The Oz" custom guitar, using Shark Tooth picks. For more details, visit:

https://www.eggle.co.uk/

http://www.strum-n-comfort.com/

Contents

About the Author

Tim Pettingale is an award-winning author, editor and guitarist who has been involved in international publishing for almost 25 years. He is the author of five bestselling jazz guitar tuition books, and has collaborated on publishing projects with some of the world's most respected players including, Mike Stern, Oz Noy, Ulf Wakenius, Robben Ford, Josh Smith, John Patitucci, Mark Whitfield, Allen Hinds, Jennifer Batten, Steve Morse and many more. He is grateful to have had not one but two great jazz guitar mentors over the years: Adrian Ingram and Dr Martin Taylor MBE.

Introduction

The concept of using substitute tonalities over chord changes is an idea that permeates the whole of modern jazz. All the jazz greats over the years have employed some "substitution thinking" to spice up their melodic lines and create interest over potentially boring harmonies, and today's leading players continue to push the envelope.

Simply put, the core idea is that when we see a chord written on a lead sheet, we can play a different chord tonality to the one written. The act of superimposing one tonality over another instantly produces a richer melodic sound that usually incorporates some extended and altered tension notes.

A substitution is a kind of "hack" that quickly produces a complex melodic sound. Why do it? Because it's easier to use something you already know in a new way than it is to master something from scratch (like an exotic altered scale). For example, you probably know your major 7 arpeggios inside out, so you don't need to learn anything new to superimpose that sound over a different chord to create some fresh, interesting sounds. Instead, you just need a guide to know which arpeggios work best in a specific context.

The importance of the V chord

Most of the time in jazz, the chord over which substitution thinking is applied is the V chord. I.e., the dominant 7 in a ii V I progression.

Why is this?

First of all, the ii and V chords make a similar sound and many jazz guitarists ignore the ii chord in favor of playing substitute V chord ideas (often over both chords).

Second, because the V chord already contains a degree of tension, as it wants to resolve to the I chord, this makes it more suitable than other chords to have its tones extended and altered to add more tension.

In this book we're going to learn how to create a whole range of new sounds by substituting different arpeggios over the V chord in the Major ii V I sequence – the most common chord progression in jazz. As a bonus, nearly all of the substitutions will work equally well over the Minor ii V I, and these ideas are demonstrated throughout.

How the material is presented

Though there is a sound theoretical explanation in music harmony for every substitution in this book, as we play through them, I'll explain them in terms of simple movements you can make on guitar (e.g. play this arpeggio a perfect 5th above, a whole step down, a minor 3rd above, etc.) This will make it easier for you to memorize the ideas and recall them in a live musical situation, where you haven't got time to think too much about theory.

To present the substitution ideas, I've grouped them together by arpeggio type:

- Minor

- Major

- Minor 7b5

- Dominant 7

For each arpeggio type we'll take the same approach:

First, I'll illustrate some useful positions to play the arpeggio, which you can refer back to when practicing.

Then, we'll look at a series of substitutions you can make using the arpeggio.

In each case we'll "audition" the sound of the substitution by playing it very simply at first, to allow the sound of the intervals sink in. (The best way to understand these ideas is to hear them for yourself and listen to the sound they make).

Then, we'll get creative and use the substitution in a series of melodic ii V I licks. The test for these substitutions is that they have to *actually sound good* in a real musical context.

By the end of the book, you'll have added lots of new ideas to your repertoire of melodic ii V I lines, but more importantly, you'll have an eye-opening musical concept to work on that will add value to your playing for years to come. I trust that exploring these substitute tonalities will inspire you to experiment further, and keep adding fresh ideas to your playing.

Now, let's dive into the music.

Get the Audio

The audio files for this book are available to download for free from **www.fundamental-changes.com.** The link is in the top right-hand corner. Click on the "Guitar" link then simply select this book title from the drop-down menu and follow the instructions to get the audio.

We recommend that you download the files directly to your computer, not to your tablet, and extract them there before adding them to your media library. You can then put them onto your tablet, iPod or burn them to CD. On the download page there are instructions and we also provide technical support via the contact form.

For over 350 Free Guitar Lessons with Videos Check Out

www.fundamental-changes.com

Join our Facebook Community of cool musicians

www.facebook.com/groups/fundamentalguitar

Instagram: **FundamentalChanges**

Chapter One: Minor Substitutions

In this chapter we're going to explore a series of V chord substitution ideas that use minor arpeggios. Below, I've chosen to illustrate the arpeggio shapes using a minor 9 arpeggio (rather than a minor 7). This is because it's a sound that is used so often in jazz, with the 9th interval adding a cool element to the sound. We might as well take advantage of that extra note.

We'll start by looking at some useful shapes for playing the arpeggio. First, the standard box position shapes, with root notes on the fifth and sixth strings.

The root notes are highlighted in the diagrams below, so you can easily transpose them around the fretboard.

The first shape we'll look at has its root note on the fifth string. We will call this *shape one*.

Minor 9 arpeggio 5th
string root

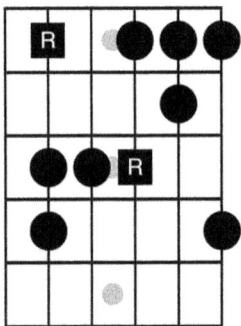

Here's how it sounds, played ascending and descending, demonstrated with a Dm9 arpeggio:

Example 1a

Shape two is the 6th string root box shape.

Minor 9 arpeggio 6th
string root

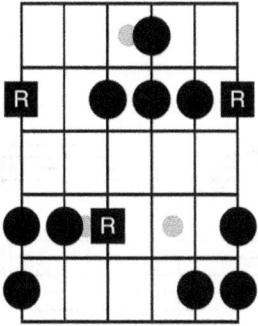

Play through the shape ascending and descending.

Example 1b

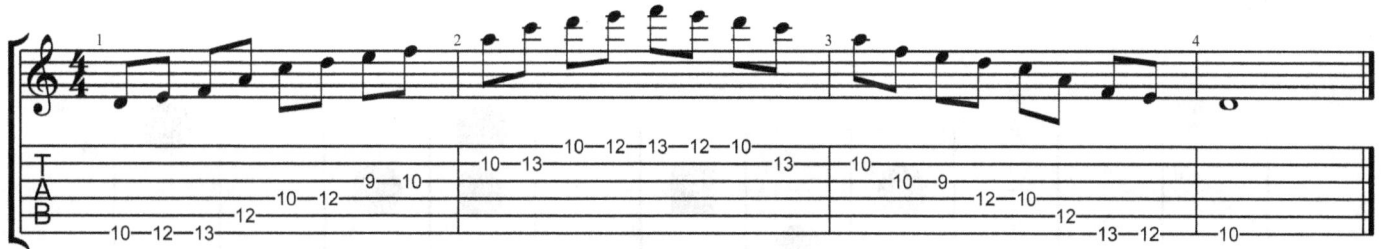

It's useful to have these box position shapes under our fingers for when we want to solo over chord changes and stay in a specific zone of the neck, but it's also useful to know arpeggio shapes across the range of the fretboard to create more exciting licks that transition between positions.

To help with this, we can learn the arpeggios as *extended* shapes that move across the neck.

Shape three is an extended minor 9 arpeggio that begins from the 5th string root and extends to the 13th fret.

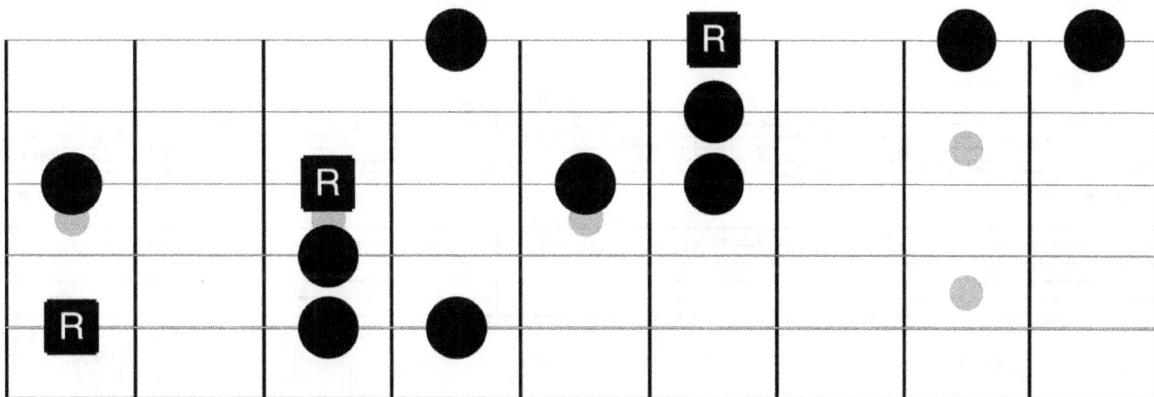

Example 1c demonstrates how this sounds, ascending and descending, with a Dm9 arpeggio.

Example 1c

```
    1                          2                          3                          4
T|------------------------------------10----------------------------------------------------------|
A|----------5--7--9--10-------------------------------10--9--7---------------------------------------|
B|--5--7--8--------------------------------------------------------10--7-----8--7----5-------------|
                           8--10--12--13--12--10--8            10
```

Notice that when ascending, playing this shape requires a quick fretting hand shift around the 10th fret, in order to be in the correct position for the notes on the top two strings. It's easier when coming back down.

This diagram approaches the sixth string root pattern in the same way. The diagram below shows the extended shape. This is *shape four*.

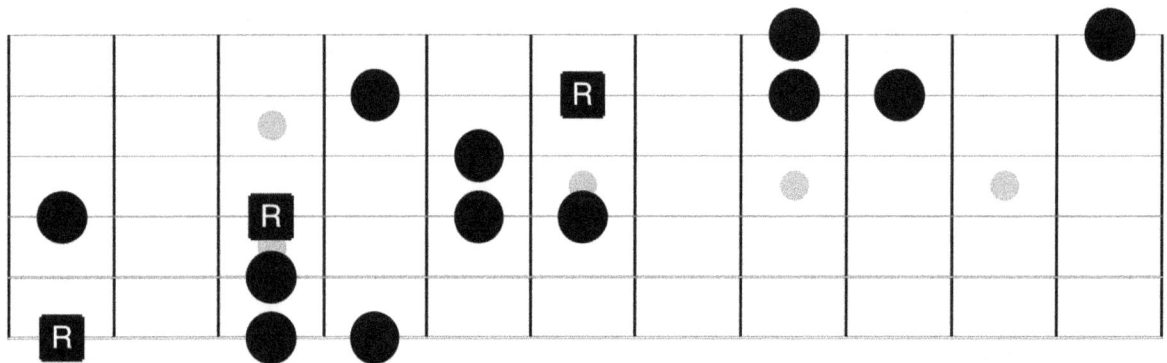

Here's how this shape sounds with a Gm9 arpeggio.

Example 1d

```
    1                          2                          3                          4
T|------------------------------------------10--13--10------------------------------------------------|
A|----------3--5--7--8--------------6--8--10--11------------11--10--8--6---------3---------------------|
B|--3--5--6--------------------7--------------------------------------------7-------5----6--5--3------|
```

These are the four basic shapes we'll use to create all the minor arpeggio licks in this chapter. Spend as much time as you can memorizing the shapes as we'll occasionally need to transpose them around the fretboard. (For a thorough arpeggio workout, check out the previous book in this series, *Jazz Guitar Arpeggio Soloing* by Fundamental Changes).

Now it's time to audition our first substitution idea. Each example in this chapter is played over a major or minor ii V I progression.

1. Minor arpeggio a perfect 5th above

The first substitution we'll test out is the simplest. We will superimpose a minor arpeggio whose root is a perfect 5th above the root of the dominant 7 chord.

We're working in the key of C Major, so our ii V I sequence is Dm7 – G7 – Cmaj7.

The minor chord a perfect 5th above G7 is Dm7 (yes, the ii chord!)

When soloing over the Major ii V I, you may already be playing a Dm7 arpeggio over the ii chord, but if you develop that idea and spell out a Dm9 arpeggio over G7, it yields some nice extended tones.

First, let's audition the sound of Dm9 superimposed over G7.

(NB: on the audio for all audition tracks, you'll hear a pause of a couple of beats between each arpeggio to allow the sound of its intervals to sink in).

Example 1e

Now let's hear the arpeggio again, this time "enclosed" by melodic phrases as part of a lick. The Dm9 arpeggio is played descending this time.

Example 1f

Now let's examine why this substitution works.

The G7 chord is constructed using the notes: G (root), B (3rd), D (5th), F (b7).

Dm9 shares two notes with G7 (D and F), then adds the notes A, C and E. These are the 9th, 11th and 13th intervals of G7. It's pretty much the perfect substitution to spell out all the extended tones of the dominant chord but contains no altered tones.

Now we've established the concept, let's use this idea to play some authentic jazz lines. The first lick uses the shape one arpeggio with the root on the fifth string root. It uses an ascending run up the arpeggio shape and combines 1/16th and 1/8th notes.

Example 1g

Now play through the next example which uses the *shape two* box position in the higher register. This lick uses the top strings to create a melodic phrase with Dm9 arpeggio notes. In bar four, after ascending a Cmaj7 arpeggio in the previous bar, the line ends on an F# tension note (implying the sound of Cmaj7#11).

Example 1h

This example uses the *shape three* extended arpeggio, built from the fifth string root note. We ascend the shape in the first half of bar two then transition into a lick for the second half.

Example 1i

Now let's try a line with *shape four*, the sixth string root extended shape. This is swinging line that makes a short motif from the Dm9 arpeggio on the top strings.

Example 1j

The arpeggio substitutions in this book will nearly always work just as well in place of the V chord in a Minor ii V i context. So, let's change key to C Minor and hear that substitution again.

This time, the chord progression will be Dm7b5 – G7b9 – Cm7 – Abmaj7 (the vi chord has been added at the end). Try the following example licks and listen to how the Dm9 arpeggio works in this slightly different context.

(NB: I won't illustrate Minor ii V i lines for every concept in this book, as space won't allow it, but you can audition every idea for yourself over the Minor ii V I backing track that comes with the free audio download).

This line begins by ascending a Dm7b5 arpeggio. In bar two, we ascend the Dm9 arpeggio, but omit the root note at the beginning.

Example 1k

Using the upper part of *shape two* to create a melodic phrase, you can hear that the Dm9 substitution instantly creates a more modern sound in a Minor ii V i context. We keep the motival idea going over the Cm11 chord.

Example 1l

This example uses the Dm9 arpeggio to create a lick that is repeated note-for-note a whole step down over the Cm11 chord in bar three.

Example 1m

In this line, C and E notes fall on the strong beats of bar two, emphasizing the 11th and 13th extended tones.

Example 1n

2. The ii chord up a whole step

The next substitution idea is to take the ii chord and move it up a whole step to superimpose it over the V chord. We're back to C Major for these examples and the ii chord is Dm7. This means that over the G7 chord, we'll play an Em9 arpeggio (a whole step up from D minor).

This is a guitar friendly substitution because it's easy to play a lick then move it up a whole step to repeat it. This can form the basis of many motif-like ideas.

First, let's hear how the substitution sounds, with Em9 superimposed over G7.

Example 1o

Now listen to the arpeggio again, enclosed by a melodic line. The Em9 arpeggio is played descending.

Example 1p

Let's take a look at why this substitution works.

Em9 shares three notes with G7 (G, B, D) and adds the notes E and F#.

We know from the previous example that the E is the 13th interval when superimposed over G7.

The F# could be considered a clash or avoid note, since it's a major 7 interval played over a chord that contains a b7. But we needn't omit it; instead it can act as a chromatic passing note. When playing melodic lines, it adds a brief dissonant tension that can be resolved up a half-step to the root of G7, or down a half-step to the b7 (F). Or, we can resolve it to a chord tone of the I chord in bar three.

Let's hear how it sounds embedded in some jazz licks.

This first line uses the G, F#, B and D notes of Em9 but omits the E root to create a descending phrase. The line ends on a Bb note in bar four (the b9 of the passing A7 chord).

Example 1q

This line begins the Em9 arpeggio on a G7 chord tone.

Example 1r

For the next two examples, we'll change key to G Major. Now, the ii V I progression will be Am7 – D7 – Gmaj7, like the opening bars of *Autumn Leaves*. We can quickly work out that we need to play a Bm9 arpeggio over the D7 chord, by visualizing the Am7 chord moved up a whole step.

Notice that compared to what we might normally play on *Autumn Leaves* the substitution immediately creates a more modern sound.

Example 1s

Here's another take on this with a contemporary twist.

Example 1t

Let's change key again to C Minor and hear a couple of examples over the Minor ii V i. This means we're back to using Em9 as our substitute arpeggio.

This example breaks up the minor 9 arpeggio rhythmically.

Example 1u

In this lick, Em9 arpeggio notes around 2nd position form the first half of the 1/16th note phrase before transitioning into a *shape one* ascending run.

Example 1v

3. Minor arpeggio a half-step above the V chord

Next we turn to one of the most well-known and often heard substitutions in jazz – the idea of superimposing a minor 9 arpeggio whose root is a half-step above the dominant chord. In C Major, this changes our standard ii V I sequence from Dm7 – G7 – Cmaj7 to Dm7 – [Abm9] – Cmaj7.

If you think you've never heard this idea before, you almost certainly have. Check out the A section to the tune *Satin Doll*. The chord changes in bars 4-7 are:

| Em7 A7 | Am7 D7 | Abm7 Db7 | Cmaj7 |

The harmony in bars 6-7 should really be,

| Dm7 G7 | Cmaj7 |

But the "minor a half-step above the V" substitution has been written into the changes as a ii V.

The next example demonstrates the sound by of this substitution by ascending each arpeggio. Play it slowly and listen carefully to the sound that the Abm9 arpeggio makes over the G7 chord. We're using the upper part of *shape two* to play the arpeggio from the fourth string.

Example 1w

Compared to the "inside" sounding Dm9 and Em9 arpeggios, Abm9 might be a shock to the ears initially, especially played as a straight ascending arpeggio, but stick with it.

Let's hear the arpeggio again, this time enclosed by melodic lines as part of a lick. As usual, the Abm9 arpeggio is played descending.

Example 1x

Why does this substitution work?

Abm9 has only one note in common with G7 (B). This means that the remaining notes that make up the chord (Ab, Eb, Gb and Bb) all create altered tensions over G7.

In turn, they are:

Ab = b9 (implies a G7b9 chord)

Eb = #5 (implies G7#5 or G7b13)

Gb (or F#) = the major 7, which can be used as a passing note as seen earlier.

Bb (or A#) = the #9 (implies G7#9)

19

Superimposing Abm9 over G7 is a great hack, because it gives you easy, immediate access to the notes of the Altered scale. Let's get creative and learn some authentic jazz licks that utilize this arpeggio.

A straight ascent of the arpeggio is effective in this example.

Example 1y

This line takes a more sequenced approach, playing the notes of the Abm9 arpeggio out of order. We're starting on the Bb note, which creates a #9 sound over G7.

Example 1z

Here's a line with a descending Abm9 arpeggio idea. The substitute line begins by alternating with a C Major scale tone (the G note is not a mistake!) before the run down.

Example 1z1

Here's a simple doubling-back idea.

Example 1z2

Let's change key and go to the relative minor key of C Major: A Minor. The Minor ii V i progression will be Bm7b5 – E7 – Am7.

Remember that we locate the minor 9 arpeggio we want to play over the E7 chord by moving up a half-step from its root, which gives us Fm9. Here are some example licks that use this Minor ii V i substitution idea. I think you'll agree that it makes a pretty cool sound.

This example works the Fm9 arpeggio hard with a 1/16th note line.

Example 1z3

Here, the substitute line in bar two echoes the phrasing of bar one.

Example 1z4

The Fm9 line in this example aims to land on its Ab note, so that it can resolve a half-step up to the root of the Am7 chord.

Example 1z5

4. Minor arpeggio a minor 3rd above the ii chord

In this next set of examples, we're going to use the Fm9 arpeggio again, but in a different context to create a different kind of sound.

We're changing key back to C Major, and this time Fm9 will substitute for the G7 chord in the Major ii V I progression.

There are two ways to remember this substitution. We can think of it as playing a minor arpeggio a whole step below the dominant chord. Or, we can view it as a minor arpeggio played a minor 3rd above the ii chord (a distance of three frets – i.e. Dm7 to Fm9).

I think of it in the latter way, because in modern jazz, it's a common idea to shift melodic ideas around in minor 3rds. In fact, if you make that minor 3rd jump, and continue to move in minor 3rds, you will eventually arrive back where you started:

Dm7 to Fm7 (minor 3rd)

Fm7 to Abm7 (minor 3rd)

Abm7 to Bm7 (minor 3rd)

Bm7 to **Dm7** (minor 3rd)

Sometimes you'll hear modern jazz improvisers cycle through these minor 3rd shifts in order to move their melodic lines away from the tonal center of the music then bring them back again. It's an important idea in jazz and a few of our substitutions stem from this core idea.

I think the minor 3rd shift creates a great sound. Let's audition it in the Major ii V I with Fm9.

Example 1z6

Let's hear the enclosed arpeggio as part of a lick.

Example 1z7

What effect does this substitution have on the harmony?

Fm9 is constructed from the notes F, Ab, C, Eb, G. It contains the root and b7 (G, F) of the G7 chord, then adds one extended tone and two altered tones.

The C note is the 11th of G7.

The Ab and Eb notes are the b9 and #5 respectively.

Play through the following licks that use this idea.

We start with a 1/16th note run where the Fm9 substitution mimics the phrasing of bar one.

Example 1z8

In this example the arpeggio is sequenced with the notes placed in a specific order, a bit like a Coltrane pattern. Over the G7 chord, the four-note phrase (F, Ab, G, C) spells out the b7, b9, root and 11th. The phrase is then repeated an octave higher. Simple phrases like this can have a great effect if the notes are chosen with care.

Example 1z9

This line takes a similar sequenced approach, beginning on the #5 / b13 tension note.

Example 1z10

This idea uses a smaller number of arpeggio notes and repeats them to create an intervallic motif.

Example 1z11

Here's another line that takes a similar approach.

Example 1z12

This substitution also works really well in a Minor ii V i setting. Let's change key to C Minor. Our progression is now Dm7b5 – G7 – Cm7. Check out the following melodic ideas.

This first idea copies the Fm9 line from the previous example, but now the context is different.

Example 1z13

Here are two more ideas to try before we move on.

Example 1z14

Example 1z15

5. Minor chord a whole step below the ii chord

The next substitution is also best remembered in relation to the ii chord of the ii V I. This time we shift *down* a whole step from Dm7 to play a Cm9 arpeggio over the G7 chord in the Major ii V I. I.e. Dm7 – [Cm9] – Cmaj7. Let's audition this sound.

Example 1z16

Let's hear the enclosed arpeggio as part of a lick.

Example 1z17

Let's look at how this substitution affects the harmony by comparing the notes of the two chords.

G7 = G, B, D, F

Cm9 = C, Eb, G, Bb, D

Cm9 has the root and 5th of G7, and adds C (11th), Eb (#5) and Bb (#9).

We're just a few examples in and you've probably noticed that each substitution idea brings a slightly different group of extended and/or altered tones. However, don't make the mistake of thinking that they all essentially do the same thing. We discover the real value of this approach when we understand that, suddenly, it opens up the whole fretboard for potential melodic ideas.

Think about the Major ii V I ideas we've played so far.

We've utilized Dm9, Em9, Abm9, Fm9, and now Cm9 arpeggios, and there's still more to come. The real benefit of this approach is that it enables us to create melodic ideas in many different zones of the fretboard, using knowledge we already possess.

Plus, we've only used *one* type of arpeggio so far. By the end of this book, you'll never be short of ideas again when you see Dm7 – G7 – Cmaj7 (or Dm7b5 – G7 – Cm7) written on a chart.

Let's try out the Cm9 arpeggio in some creative licks. Here's a question and answer phrase line to begin.

Example 1z18

This idea uses two different four-note descending forms of the Cm9 arpeggio.

Example 1z19

This example plays the substitute Cm9 in the same position as the Cmaj7 arpeggio that follows, to highlight the altered sound.

Example 1z20

If you were to view the Cm9 arpeggio as a map across the whole fretboard (which I highly recommend you do for any arpeggio, using a free online tool), you would see patterns of clusters of notes. See the Cm9 fretboard map below. You can immediately spot triad patterns and groups of notes that can be used like scale patterns.

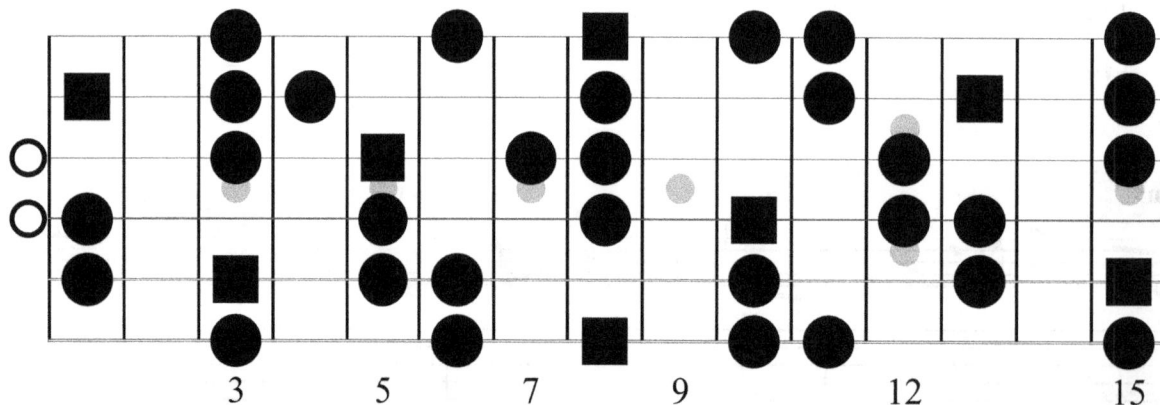

For this lick I've grouped together Cm9 arpeggio notes and played them as triads, ascending the neck. Spend some time experimenting with this idea when you practice.

Example 1z21

I won't demonstrate any Minor ii V i licks for this substitution, because it's the only one where, in the minor context, the substitute is the same as the I chord.

6. Minor arpeggio a b5 above the V chord

Many substitution ideas in this book can be considered as b5 substitutes (tritone substitutions) and here is the first. Here you'll play a minor arpeggio a flat fifth interval above the root of the dominant chord. I.e., a b5 above G7 is Dbm7.

You can also view this as the Dm7 ii chord moved down by a half-step. Go for whichever way you feel is easier to remember. It's another easy movement on guitar and lends itself to the idea of playing a lick, then repeating it note-for-note a half-step below.

Audition the sound with the example below.

Example 1z22

Now let's hear the arpeggio played descending as part of a lick. This phrase is trickier to play than previous ideas and uses a 1/16th note descending pattern for the Dbm9 arpeggio.

Example 1z23

Superimposed over G7, the Dbm9 arpeggio gives us a rich combination of extended and altered tones. The chord is spelled Db, E, Ab, B, Eb, and over G7 the intervals imply the #11, 13th, b9, 3rd and #5 respectively.

It's a modern sounding substitution and one that can be easily accessed with the side-stepping movements favored by many modern players (such as Oz Noy – a great exponent of this technique).

Now let's learn some creative licks with this substitution.

Here's a very simple side-stepping lick that repeats the phrase of bar one note for note.

Example 1z24

In this example, gentle swinging phrases are punctuated with a fast run up and down the *Shape one* minor 9 pattern.

Example 1z25

In this more intervallic example, we make use of 5th and 4th intervals to give the Dbm9 arpeggio a more modern sound.

Example 1z26

At the risk of stating the obvious, the great thing about this arpeggio substitution is that any lick we play can be resolved with a half-step movement back inside the C Major scale – which makes it a very useful tool for creating tension and resolution.

In this example, although the Dbm9 lick begins on its B note (the 3rd of G7), this line brings out the #5 and #11 character of the arpeggio, so sounds quite tense.

Example 1z27

I won't demonstrate any Minor ii V i variations here, but you can try this for yourself using the backing track. In a Minor ii V I setting, you'll discover that the side-stepping approach works in another way. In C Minor, our progression would be Dm7b5 – G7 – Cm7. With the substitution in place, that becomes Dm7b5 – [Dbm9] – Cm7. In other words, any minor lick you play using Dbm9 can be moved down a half-step and repeated over Cm7.

7. Minor arpeggio a minor 3rd above the V chord

The final minor substitution is to play the minor arpeggio a minor third above the dominant chord. Remember, that's a distance of three frets: G7 to Bbm7.

First, let's audition the sound it makes.

Example 1z28

Now let's hear it as part of a lick.

Example 1z29

This is another substitution that is a quick route to altered tensions. Bbm9 is constructed as follows, with the tensions implied over G7 in parentheses:

Bb (#9), Db (#11), F (b7), Ab (b9), C (11th)

To close out the chapter, here are four creative licks to learn which utilize this substitution.

First up is the kind of sequenced line that I love about Kurt Rosenwinkel's playing.

Example 1z30

Here's a simpler idea with two four-note phrases using Bbm9 arpeggio notes.

Example 1z31

This lick shows how to move into and out of the Bbm9 substitute arpeggio with half-step movements.

Example 1z32

The main idea in this doubling-back melodic idea is to use the Bbm9 arpeggio notes on the top string.

Example 1z33

Try this one out in a Minor ii V i setting using the backing track. Played over Dm7b5 – G7 – Cm7, you'll discover that two serendipitous things occur.

First, playing in 5th position on the neck, the arpeggios for Dm7b5 and Bbm9 are located very close together, so it's easy to slip between one and the other. Secondly, we can make a nice whole step motion between Bbm9 and Cm7.

Okay, I can't resist, here is just one Minor ii V i lick that uses this idea!

Example 1z34

In this chapter we've learned to apply a range of minor 9 arpeggio substitutions to spice up the standard ii V I progression and create a range of new sonic ideas. In a later chapter, we'll take things a step further by combining arpeggios within a single lick, but first we need to learn to apply some other arpeggio flavors.

Chapter Two: Major Substitutions

In the previous chapter we established our working method for applying chord substitutions:

- Audition the arpeggio to get the sound of its intervals in our ears

- Use it as part of a lick

- Learn creative licks using the substitute arpeggio

Previously we looked at several different ways to use the minor 9 arpeggio as a substitute to create a range of new sounds. Next, we're going to explore the potential of using the major 7 arpeggio.

The major 7 arpeggio is probably very familiar to you but let's remind ourselves of two common position-based shapes to play it, and two extended shapes that use the range of the neck. Root notes are indicated in the diagram so you can easily transpose them.

Shape one has its root note on the fifth string.

Major 7 arpeggio 5th string root

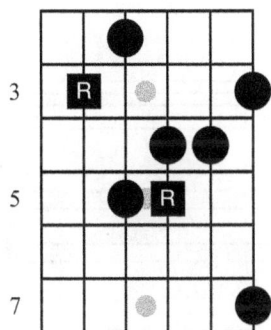

It's not strictly a box shape because it requires a position shift and a slight stretch to repeat the arpeggio in the higher register. My recommended fingering is to play the root note with the second finger. Play the first three notes in this position, then quickly move your hand to play the 4th fret on the third string with the first finger. This should allow for a very smooth ascent. Do the reverse on the descent.

Play the arpeggio ascending and descending, demonstrated here with a Cmaj7 arpeggio.

Example 2a

Shape two has its root note on the sixth string.

Major 7 arpeggio 6th
string root

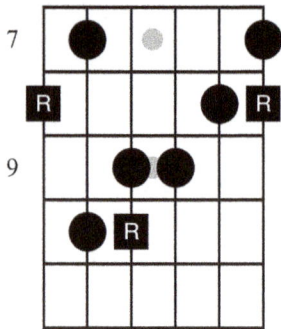

This is a true box position shape and doesn't require the fretting hand to move out of position. Play this Cmaj7 arpeggio ascending and descending and aim for a smooth, flowing arpeggiation.

Example 2b

Now let's look at two extended arpeggio shapes that offer more neck coverage. First, an extended shape built from the fifth string root note.

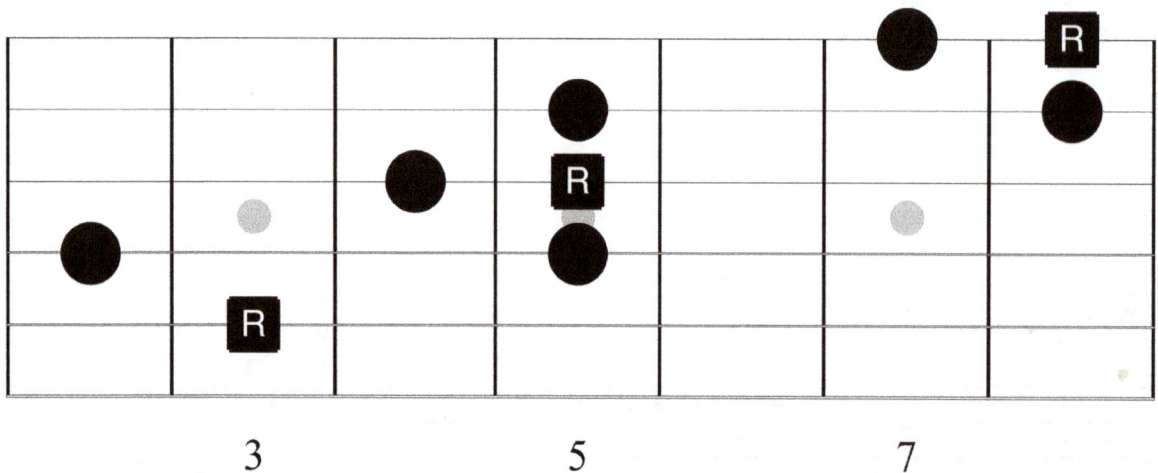

You may find it easier to use this shape with its arrangement of two notes on most strings. This Cmaj7 arpeggio is best played using two fretting hand position shifts. Begin with your second finger and shift to the 4th position again on the first B in bar one. For the B at the end of bar one, shift to 7th position and play it with the first finger.

Example 2c

```
                                    7     8  7
                          5   8           8   5
                      4  5                    5   4
              2   5                               5   2
      3                                                   3   2
```

Next is the sixth string root extended shape.

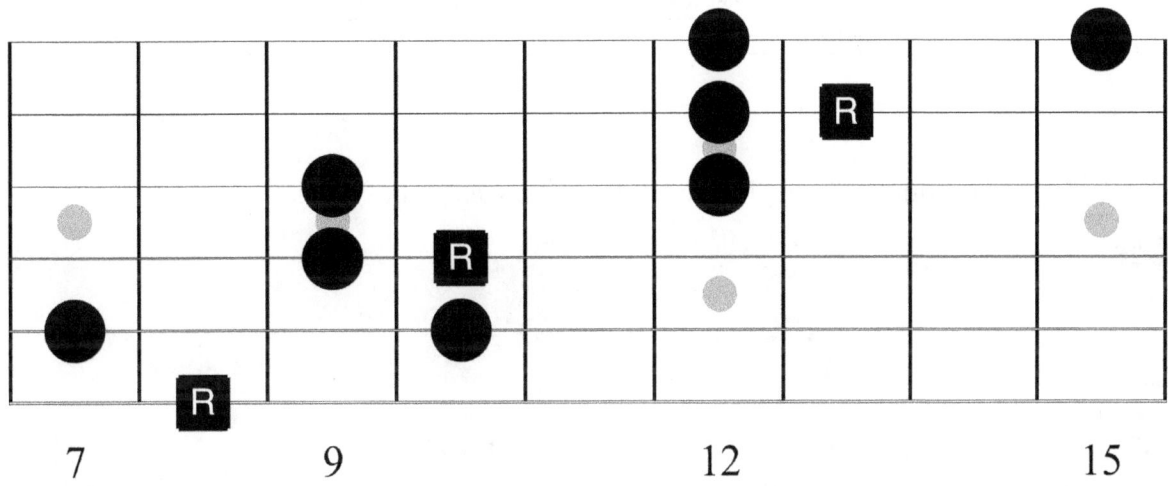

Again, demonstrated with a Cmaj7 arpeggio, this extended shape also requires two fretting hand shifts to play smoothly. I recommend beginning with your second finger and moving to 9th position for the B note on the fourth string, 9th fret. Shift to the 12th position for the final B note of bar one.

Example 2d

```
                                   12  15  12
                          12    13          13  12
                      9  12                     12   9
              9   10
          7  10                                       10   9
      8                                                       10   7
                                                                  8
```

These four shapes will be the basis for the licks we create in this chapter. Now let's see how we can use the familiar major 7 arpeggio in some new ways.

1. Major 7 arpeggio a whole step below the V chord

The first substitution we'll audition is to play a major 7 arpeggio a whole step below the root of the V chord. In the key of C Major our ii V I is Dm7 – G7 – Cmaj7. Moving a whole step below G7 leads us to an Fmaj7 arpeggio.

Here's how the substitution sounds over the G7 chord, with each arpeggio played ascending.

Example 2e

Let's hear the idea again, with the arpeggio played descending as part of a lick.

Example 2f

Let's look at the effect of this superimposition. The root note of the Fmaj7 arpeggio is the b7 interval of G7. The rest of its notes all imply extended tones:

F (b7), A (9th), C (11), E (13)

This makes it the perfect arpeggio to spell out the upper extensions of the dominant V chord, and we've already noted that it leads us to play in different areas of the fretboard than we would normally.

Now let's use this idea in some authentic jazz licks.

To kick things off, here's a 1/16th note line that uses *shape one* for the Fmaj7 line in bar two.

Example 2g

This substitute line is achieved by mixing up the order of notes in *shape one*.

Example 2h

The next line showcases the fifth string root extended major 7 pattern. To keep things interesting, bar two is made up of two seven-note 1/16th phrases, interrupted by an 1/8th note rest, which means the second half of the lick sits differently rhythmically.

Example 2i

We can create short arpeggio licks by restricting ourselves to one area of the neck and working with the notes to make a sequence, as in bar two here, where the line is arranged on the top three strings in 5th position.

Example 2j

Before we move on, let's apply this substitution to the Minor ii V i sequence, changing key to C Minor. Our progression is now Dm7b5 – G7 – Cm7. As with some of the ideas in the previous chapter, you'll discover that the Fmaj7 arpeggio is located in the same region of the fretboard where you'll play your C minor ideas, which makes it incredibly convenient for playing smooth lines that move through the changes.

Here's how this idea can work in practice.

Example 2k

This line uses the same extended arpeggio shape to move from 8th position into the higher range of the neck, where an Ebmaj7 arpeggio is played over the Cm11 chord.

Example 2l

Dm7♭5   **G7♭9**   **Cm11**

```
                                               8-12-10     10-11-10        10-13-10
                                        10                  11          11
                 6--9         10                   9-10        12          12
          7--5        10                      7-10                13-12-13
       6                 10             8--7--8
    5
```

In this example, a riff-like motif is created with the Fmaj7 arpeggio, alternating two arpeggio notes at the beginning of each phrase.

Example 2m

Dm7♭5   **G7♭9**   **Cm11**

```
                  8-10-8    12-13-12      8-12-8       5--8--5
              9               13                10             6     8
           8-10                  14              10
         10
       8--11
```

Here's a laid-back lick that starts the Fmaj7 arpeggio phrase on its E note (the 13th of G7) and ends on C (the 11th of G7).

Example 2n

Dm7♭5   **G7♭9**   **Cm11**

```
                                                   5--6--5--6    8     11-10-7--8
                               2--5                              8
             3       3--6--5              2--3
          5       5
```

2. Major 7 arpeggio a half-step above the ii chord

The next substitution idea is to play a major 7 arpeggio a half-step above the ii chord. This means that an Ebmaj7 arpeggio will replace the G7 in the Major ii V I progression. It's another guitar-friendly idea, where we can play around a D minor arpeggio shape then side-step upwards into Ebmaj7. Let's hear how this idea sounds.

Example 2o

Here's the arpeggio descending, played as part of a lick.

Example 2p

Ebmaj7 contains the notes Eb, G, Bb, D. It has two chord tones in common with G7 (G root and D, 5th). The Eb note implies the #5 interval over G7 and Bb is the #9. The substitution has a nice combination of grounded chord tones and altered tones, which make it a very useful device.

Here are some creative jazz lines that apply this substitution.

Bar two of this example begins the Ebmaj7 substitute phrase on a D note (5th) then alternates with an Eb (the tense sounding #5). The line ends on Bb (#9). Similar phrasing in each bar glues the idea together.

Example 2q

Here's a *shape one* substitution idea in bar two. The phrasing throughout this lick is structured to cross the bar line, aiming for a target note.

Example 2r

This example uses the Ebmaj7 arpeggio sequenced in 3rds. Ebmaj7 is spelled Eb, G, Bb, D, so here we play it Eb, Bb, G, D, then repeat the pattern an octave higher. Again, we start on the #5 interval.

Example 2s

The next idea is a simple line that uses identical phrasing for each bar, with the substitute line adding a richness of sound to the G7 chord.

Example 2t

Dm9   G7♭9   Cmaj7

Next, some licks that use this substitution in the Minor ii V i context. We can structure some great lines in this context that utilize the half-step root movement from Dm7b5 to Ebmaj7.

You'll no doubt also realize that Ebmaj7 is a great substitute for Cm7 (Eb Major being the relative major key to C Minor), which means we can continue to develop Ebmaj7 ideas over bars two and three.

The next three examples take this approach.

Example 2u

Dm7♭5   G7♭9   Cm11

Example 2v

Dm7♭5   G7♭9   Cm11

Dm7♭5   G7♭9   Cm11

3. Major 7 arpeggio a half-step above the V chord

Next up is an interesting variation on a substitution idea we looked at in Chapter One. Previously, we played a minor 9 arpeggio a half-step above the dominant V chord to invoke the sound of the Altered scale. Can we also use a *major 7* arpeggio in the same way? Absolutely! This is one of Kurt Rosenwinkel's favorite substitutions; in place of the G7 chord we'll play an Abmaj7 arpeggio.

First, let's audition this idea.

Example 2x

Dm7   G7♭9   Cmaj7

And now as part of a melodic lick.

Example 2y

Dm7   G7♭9   Cmaj7

Now let's look at the effect this substitution has on the underlying harmony.

Abmaj7 contains the notes Ab, C, Eb, G. In turn, these imply the b9, 11, #5 and root of the G7 chord. If you like, you can extend this arpeggio and turn it into an Abmaj9 by adding a Bb note. Over G7, the Bb adds a #9 sound.

Let's hear how it sounds in action. First, two licks that use a straight Abmaj7 arpeggio.

Example 2z

Example 2z1

Now, two licks that include the additional Bb note to make an Abmaj9 arpeggio.

Example 2z2

Example 2z3

Let's try this idea over the Minor ii V i sequence: Dm7b5 – G7 – Cm7.

Example 2z4

Example 2z5

4. Major 7 arpeggio a b5 above the V chord

The next substitution concept is another b5 idea. In Chapter One we used Dbm9 as a substitution for G7, and here we'll use its major equivalent. Our Dm7 – G7 – Cmaj7 progression now becomes Dm7 – [Dbmaj7] – Cmaj7.

Here's the audition example for this sound.

Example 2z6

And now as part of a lick.

Example 2z7

Remember our G7 chord tones: G, B, D, F. Dbmaj7 is constructed Db, F, Ab, C.

In order, they are the #11, b7, b9 and 11th intervals of G7.

Superimposing Dbmaj7 over G7 is an attention-grabbing idea because beginning on the #11 of the G7 chord is a more challenging, outside sound. This first idea does just that. For the Dbmaj7 arpeggio, we're playing a "212" shape from the 5th string root (i.e. two notes on a string, one note on the next string, two on the next, etc).

Example 2z8

Now try this more intervallic line.

Example 2z9

You can add an Eb note to the Dbmaj7 arpeggio to turn it into Dbmaj9. Over G7, Eb is the #5 interval, so we now have #11, b9 and #5 altered tones at our disposal. Listen to the difference it makes.

Example 2z10

Example 2z11

5. Major 7 arpeggio a minor third above the V chord

The final substitution idea for this chapter is to play a major 7 arpeggio a minor third (three frets) above the dominant V chord. We used this idea in Chapter One with a Bbm9 arpeggio, and once again we see that its major equivalent works equally well.

Listen to the intervals that Bbmaj7 creates when layered over the G7 chord.

Example 2z12

And again, in the context of a simple lick.

Example 2z13

Now let's learn some creative lines.

Playing in the middle zone of the neck makes it easy to transition between a D minor arpeggio, the substitute Bbmaj7 arpeggio, and the C Major scale. The last note of bar two is a chromatic passing note used to connect the arpeggio with the C Major scale.

Example 2z14

This swinging line uses approach notes a half-step below chord tones to outline the Dm7 chord. After playing the Bbmaj7 arpeggio shape in the second half of bar two, hold the shape and quickly slide it up two frets to play the Cmaj7 arpeggio.

Example 2z15

In this line, the substitute Bbmaj7 arpeggio begins on D and ends on F – both chord tones of G7. In between, 9th and #9 tones add color and tension.

Example 2z16

To close out this chapter, let's hear the same substitution in the Minor ii V i context: Dm7b5 – G7 – Cm7.

This lick is all about the 9th/#9 interplay in bar two.

Example 2z17

Here's one final example to wrap up this chapter. This modern line takes a more intervallic approach. In bar one, two arpeggiated inversions of Ddim7 are used to imply the sound of the Dm7b5 chord. In bar two, the substitute arpeggio begins in a normal descending pattern, but moves towards an intervallic arrangement at the end of the bar. Over Cm11 we make use of 4th intervals to end on an unresolved sound.

Example 2z18

Chapter Three: Minor 7b5 Substitutions

In this chapter we turn to the minor 7b5 arpeggio, otherwise known as the half-diminished. It's often used in the context of the Minor ii V i progression, to spell out the sound of the ii chord, but has many uses as a substitution, as we'll see here.

Let's look at the essential shapes we need to know to play this arpeggio.

Here is *shape one* with the root note on the fifth string.

Minor 7b5 arpeggio 5th
string root

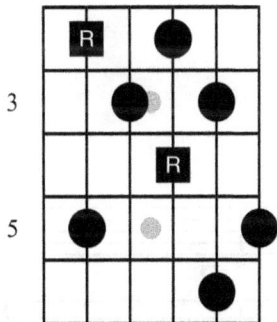

Example 3a shows *shape one* played ascending and descending demonstrated with a Bm7b5 arpeggio.

Example 3a

Next, we have *shape two* with the root note on the sixth string.

Minor 7b5 arpeggio 6th
string root

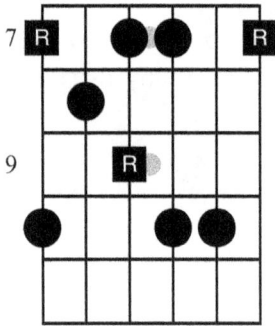

Here's a Bm7b5 arpeggio using this shape.

Example 3b

This is a common box position shape but there is an alternative way to play it. This variation is another "212" shape, favored by players like Tim Miller and Greg Howe.

This shape eliminates the awkward parallel notes at the 10th fret of the box shape, that have to be played with the fourth finger. Although there is more of a stretch on the second string, it's worth doing because the arpeggio flows much better across the strings.

Example 3c

Now let's look at two extended shapes for this arpeggio using the Bm7b5 arpeggio. First, *Shape three* from the fifth string root note.

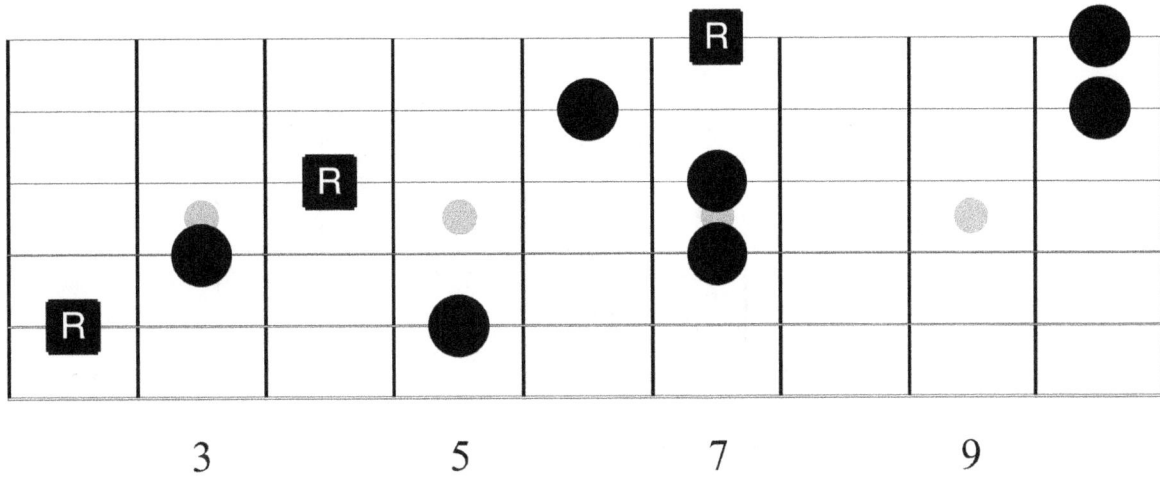

Example 3d

The interval layout of this arpeggio makes for some bigger stretches when extending it across the fretboard, so if you prefer not to stretch too far, here's an alternative shape that relies on sliding between positions instead.

Example 3e

Now we move on to the sixth string root extended *shape four.*

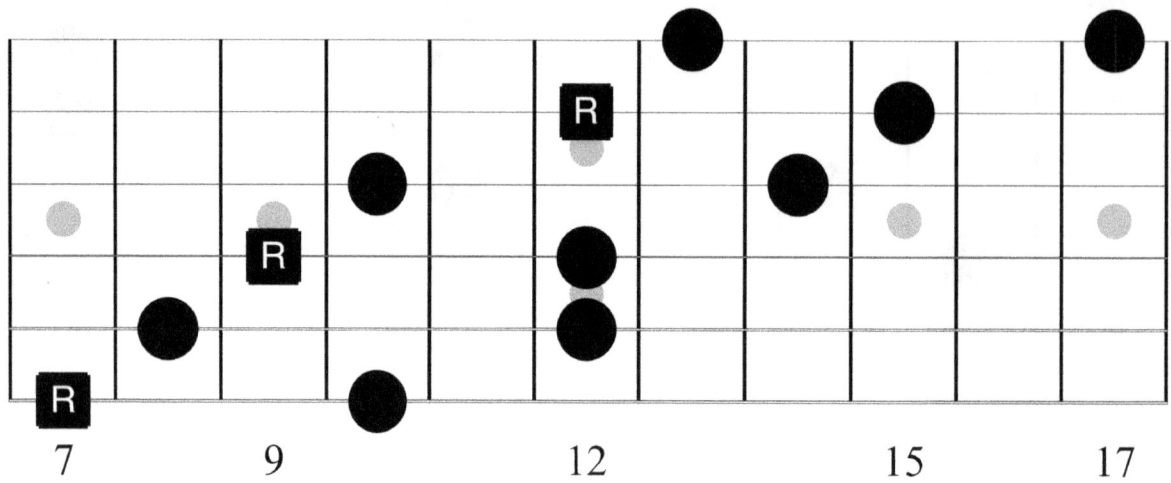

Example 3f

While the stretches are easily achievable in this region of the neck, for arpeggios in other positions there is an alternative shape that includes a position slide. It omits the high A note of the Bm7b5 arpeggio.

Example 3g

The minor 7b5 arpeggio is not a go-to shape for many players, so take some time to practice these patterns and get the sound/shape of the intervals in your ears before moving on. When you feel comfortable with the shapes, look at how this arpeggio can be used to create some interesting melodic ideas in the following licks.

1. Minor 7b5 a 3rd above the dominant chord

The first idea we'll look at is to play a minor 7b5 arpeggio from the 3rd of the dominant V chord. The 3rd of G7 is B, so the superimposed arpeggio will be Bm7b5.

Bm7b5 is also chord vii of the parent key, C Major. Let's hear how this sounds.

Example 3h

Now, as part of a melodic phrase.

Example 3i

Bm7b5 is constructed B, D, F, A. It contains the 3rd, 5th and b7 of G7 and adds the 9th. It therefore creates a very safe, inside sounding harmony, but works well because it avoids the root of the dominant chord and adds the spacious sounding 9th.

Playing a sequenced Bm7b5 arpeggio over G7 is a very effective soloing tool as we'll see in the examples that follow.

This first example descends and doubles back through *shape one* of the Bm7b5 arpeggio, beginning on the 9th of G7.

Example 3j

The next lick uses the top part of *shape three* to form a descending melody (relocating the F note from the second string, 6th fret, to the third string, 10th fret, to keep the line in the same zone).

Example 3k

Here's a rhythmically broken line that uses an extended *shape four* from the sixth string root.

Example 3l

This lick forms a melodic line around the *shape two* minor 7b5 box position.

Example 3m

2. Minor 7b5 a 5th above the dominant chord

The next substitution is to play a minor 7b5 arpeggio a 5th above the dominant V chord. In other words, we're building the arpeggio from the 5th of G7 (D). G7 = Dm7b5.

Let's audition that sound.

Example 3n

And again, as a melodic phrase.

Example 3o

Dm7b5 has the notes D, F, Ab, C. This is an interesting substitution because we can play it with minimal movement on guitar. For example, we might play a D minor 7 arpeggio over the ii chord, then we can flatten one note (A to Ab) to continue the idea over the V chord and spell out some richer intervals.

In order, the notes imply the 5th, b7, b9 and 11th over G7. Two chord tones connect the harmony to G7, then the b9 is a very popular note choice for a dominant chord in bebop, and the 11th adds some tension.

Check out the following licks.

The first example breaks up the rhythm of a Dm7 arpeggio in bar one, then uses the fifth string root shape of Dm7b5 to descend the arpeggio. Because both lines are played in the same zone of the neck, the note differences of each arpeggio stand out.

Example 3p

Here, the notes of Dm7b5 are sequenced to create a descending 1/8th note triplet line. The ends on the Ab note, which resolves neatly to the G scale tone of C Major.

Example 3q

The next line is another simple sequencing idea that mixes up the order of the Dm7b5 arpeggio notes to create a melody.

Example 3r

In bar one of this idea, notes of the C Major scale ascend on the first string, doubling back on themselves. For the substitute Dm7b5 line, a 1/16th rhythmic motif creates interest and dovetails, via a half-step movement, back into C Major in bar three.

Example 3s

3. Minor 7b5 a whole step below the V chord

I've called this substitution a whole step movement down from the dominant V chord. It is, of course, an arpeggio beginning on the b7 (F) of G7, but thinking of it as a whole step down is easier to remember and transpose to other dominant chords. So, this time we are superimposing Fm7b5 over G7. Here is how that sounds:

Example 3t

Let's audition it in a straightforward lick.

Example 3u

This substitution works because it contains two chord tones and two altered tones. Fm7b5 has the notes F, Ab, B and Eb, in turn the b7, b9, 3rd and #5 (or b13).

In the first example of this substitution, 4th intervals are used to spell out the D minor chord in bar one. In bar two, the line takes advantage of the fact that superimposing an Fm7b5 arpeggio over G7 makes a G7#5b9 sound. The first four notes are a rootless voicing of this chord.

Example 3v

Here's a line that use two descending forms of Fm7b5 to spell out the G7 altered sound.

Example 3w

This line makes a feature of the #5 and b9 tension notes by playing both on adjacent strings twice in this lick in bar two.

Example 3x

And now, a line that uses two ascending forms of Fm7b5

Example 3y

4. Minor 7b5 a whole step above the V chord

For the next substitution we move in the opposite direction, to play a minor 7b5 arpeggio a whole step *above* the dominant V chord. This time G7 = Am7b5 to provide material for our melodic lines.

Play through the audition lick and listen to the sound of the intervals over the G7 chord.

Example 3z

Now try this idea as part of a lick.

Example 3z1

Am7b5 (A, C, Eb, G) shares just one note with G7 – the root. The remaining chord tones represent the 9th, 11th and #5, so this substitution creates a nice tense outside sound, which makes it very effective in producing some modern sounding licks.

This line launches the first four-note Am7b5 phrase from the #5, and the second from the 9th.

Example 3z2

Here's another intervallic lick that mixes 5th and 4th intervals.

Example 3z3

Next is a 1/16th note sequenced run using the Am7b5 arpeggio. The fingering is a bit tricky here. After playing the first four notes, your fourth finger should be on the first string, 5th fret. Now jump your first finger over onto the 7th fret of the fourth string to begin the next four note phrase. Once the first finger is in place, it's easy to roll the second finger onto the top three strings to play the 8th fret notes. Play the remaining notes in bar two as you would a descending pentatonic-style lick with pull-offs.

Example 3z4

The final Am7b5 example shows how we can achieve a lot with very simple phrasing if we choose the notes carefully.

Example 3z5

5. Minor 7b5 a minor 3rd below the V chord

The final minor 7b5 idea we'll look at is to play an arpeggio a minor 3rd below the dominant V chord. From the root of the dominant, walk down three frets. From G7, that gives us Em7b5. If you prefer, think of the substitute as being a whole step above the ii chord (Dm7 to Em7b5). Whichever way helps you to remember it is best! Here's how the substitution sounds.

Example 3z6

Now let's audition it with a simple lick.

Example 3z7

Emb75 is built from the notes E, G, Bb and D. The effect of this substitution over G7 is two shared notes (G and D, root and 5th), an extended note (E, 13th) and one altered note (Bb, #9).

This line rearranges the order of the arpeggio notes to Bb, G, E, D, which creates an easy descending pattern on the top two strings. It also means the lick begins on the altered #9 tone. This pattern is repeated an octave lower.

Example 3z8

In the next example, the phrases in bars one and two are played in the same zone of the fretboard, so it's easy to hear the extended/altered notes of the Em7b5 standing out.

Example 3z9

Dm9   G7♭9   Cmaj7

Here's a modern sounding intervallic arrangement of the arpeggio in bar two. The fingering is tricky at speed, so work out the most economical way of playing it that works for you, taking it slowly to begin with.

Example 3z10

Dm9   G7♭9   Cmaj7

Here's one final idea for this chapter. Remember that you can also use *all* the substitutions in this chapter in a Minor ii V i setting. Try them out over the minor backing track.

Example 3z11

Dm9   G7♭9   Cmaj7

Chapter Four: Dominant 7 Substitutions

When you've been playing the jazz repertoire for a while, and built a foundational understanding of the chord progressions that crop up time and again, you begin to notice two things:

1. How often dominant chords are used as chord substitutions.

2. How often the *quality* of any chord is changed to a dominant chord (usually from a minor chord).

For an example of a dominant chord substitution look at the tune *Stella by Starlight*. In bars 4-8 the chord changes typically written are:

| Fm7 | Bb7 | Ebmaj7 | Ab7 |

In the original score for the tune, the Ab7 chord is written as Ebm6. Compare the notes of Ebm6 and Ab7 and you'll see why this substitution works:

Ebm6 = Eb, Gb, Bb, C

Ab7 = Ab, C, Eb, Gb

The chords share three notes in common. In fact, if you choose to play an Ab13 here, you'll have *all* the notes of Ebm6, plus a couple of extra tones.

This particular movement is one that crops up in many different tunes and the reason for it is simply that there is more scope to layer extended or altered tones on top of a dominant chord.

For an example of changing the *quality* of a chord to a dominant, look at *The Girl from Ipanema*. The first eight bars read as follows:

| Fmaj7 | % | G7 | % |

| Gm7 | Gb7 | Fmaj7 | Gb7 |

In the key of F Major, chord ii should be Gm7, but in bar three it's written as G7 (sometimes rendered G7#11). The plain sounding ii chord has been turned into a dominant to make the harmony richer.

These bars also contain a dominant chord substitution. According to the parent key of the tune, bar six should read C7 – the V chord that will resolve to the I, Fmaj7. Instead, we have Gb7, a b5 substitution.

These two simple changes totally transform this piece of music, but as we've seen throughout this book, we can play these ideas melodically, even if the chords presented to us are the plain, vanilla version.

Let's learn the four essential shapes for the dominant 7 arpeggio and begin to apply some of these ideas.

Shape one has its root note on the fifth string.

Dominant 7 arpeggio 5th
string root

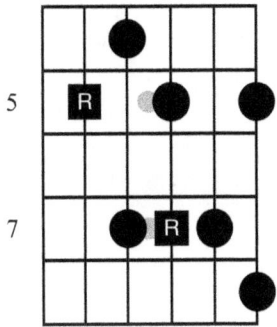

Here's how it sounds, played ascending and descending, demonstrated with a D7 arpeggio:

Example 4a

There is an alternative way to play the arpeggio in this position that just falls nicely on the fretboard. It uses notes below the root to complete the shape.

Example 4b

Shape two has its root note on the sixth string.

Dominant 7 arpeggio 6th
string root

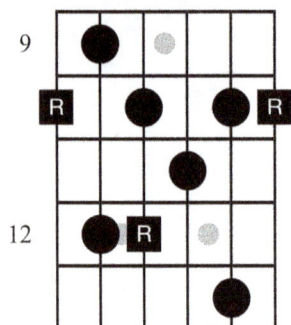

Example 4c

We can apply a similar alternative pattern to this shape too, and play it like this:

Example 4d

Now let's look at two extended patterns for the dominant 7 arpeggio.

First, *shape three* is the extended fifth string root pattern.

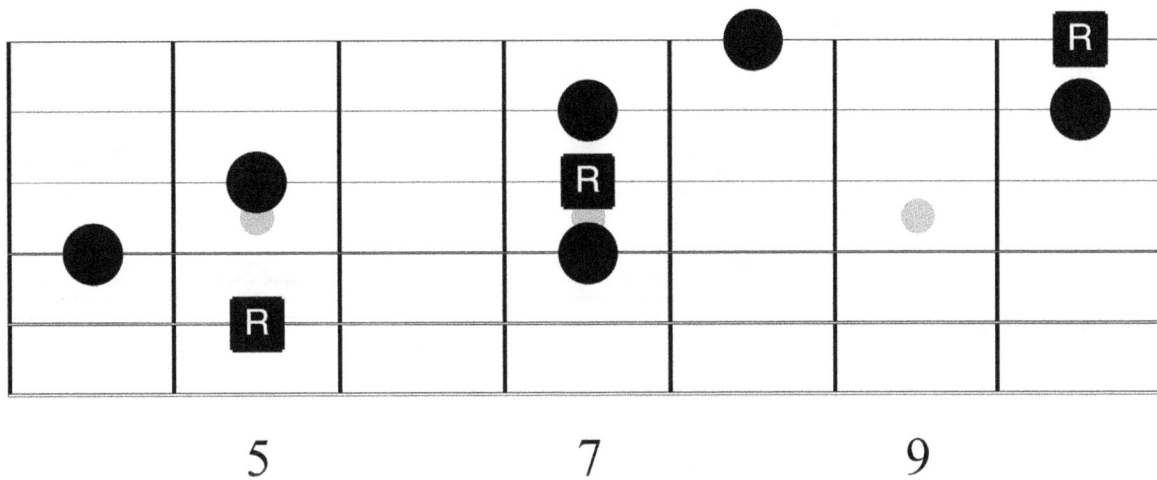

Example 4e

Shape four is the extended sixth string root pattern. For this example, we'll switch to a G7 chord. If we used the D7 to demonstrate, it would take us up to the 20th fret, which on most jazz guitars is impractical.

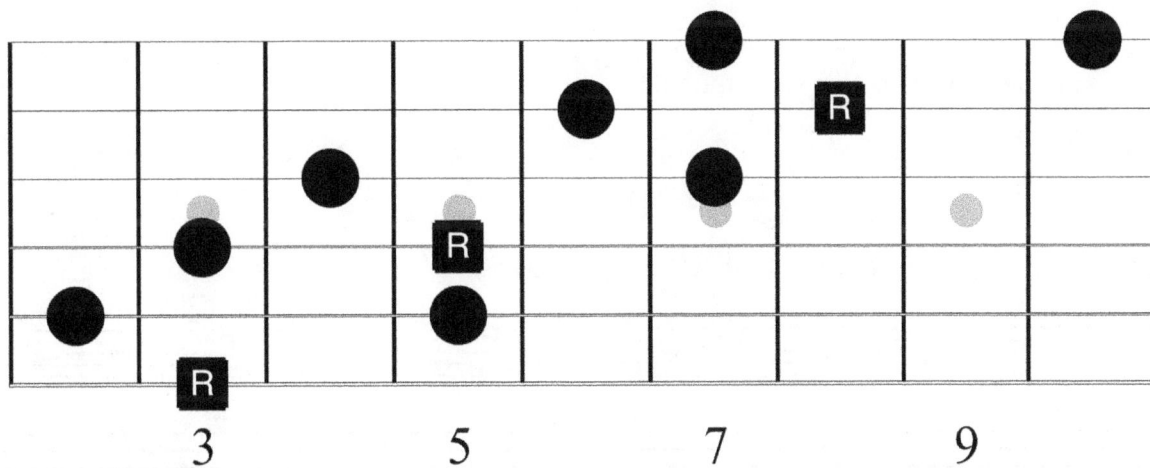

Example 4f

Practice the shapes to get really familiar with them. Now, let's move on to the substitution ideas.

1. Dominant 7 arpeggio a b5 above the V chord

To begin our dominant chord substitution ideas, here is the most common: to substitute the dominant V chord with another dominant chord a b5 above it. In C Major, this means playing a Db7 arpeggio over the G7 chord. Let's audition this sound.

Example 4g

Now, here is a simple line using this substitution.

Example 4h

This substitution works well because it contains two of the most important tones that define the sound of G7, the 3rd and b7. Then it adds two altered notes. Here are the chord tones of Db7, with the intervals created over G7 in parentheses:

Db7 = Db (#11), F (b7), Ab (b9), B (3rd)

It's ideal for instantly creating the G7b9 sound, but also brings the tense sound of the #11 into the equation. Let's apply this idea in some licks.

The first idea here begins on the b9 note to play a repeating motif.

Example 4i

Next, a much more laidback line that makes a feature of the b9 and #11 tension notes.

Example 4j

Here is another line that leads with the #11 and b9 tones and ends on the B note of Db7, which also happens to be the 7th of Cmaj7.

Example 4k

The next idea sequences the substitute Db7 arpeggio in 3rds (i.e. beginning on the Db note then skipping alternate notes).

Example 4l

2. Dominant 7 arpeggio a half-step above the ii chord

The next substitution is best thought of as a half-step movement above the ii chord. In C Major, that's the movement from Dm7 to Eb7.

Here's how it sounds.

Example 4m

Now audition the sound in the context of an easy lick.

Example 4n

This time, the substitute arpeggio contains the root of the G7 chord, plus three altered tones. They are perhaps the tensest sounding combination we've used so far.

Eb7 = Eb (#5), G (root), Bb (#9), Db (#11)

Let's hear this substitution in action.

Here's a simple but effective idea that uses question and answer phrasing. The substitute Eb7 lick leads and ends with the #9 altered tone.

Example 4o

In bar two of this example, we lead off with the G note of the Eb7 substitute arpeggio, and the G is repeated at the end of the first four-note phrase. Referencing the root note of the underlying G7 twice like this, helps our ears to accept the tense altered tones that accompany it.

Example 4p

When improvising with arpeggios, I always recommend using some free online software to "map" the whole fretboard with the arpeggio notes. Having box shapes to fall back on is always helpful, but mapping the neck immediately reveals the patterns that lie hidden within the arpeggio's geography.

If you know the notes of the fretboard inside out, you may have come to an idea like the following yourself, but it's much easier to visualize with a fretboard map.

Example 4q

Here's a similar intervallic motif with the Eb7 arpeggio in bar two.

Example 4r

3. Dominant 7 arpeggio a half-step above the V chord

The next idea is to play a dominant 7 arpeggio a half-step above the original V chord: from G7 to Ab7. We've already heard minor and major variations of this idea, now here is the dominant 7 equivalent. First, we'll audition the sound in simple form.

Example 4s

And as part of a simple lick.

Example 4t

Ab7 is constructed Ab, C, Eb, Gb. Played over G7, it implies b9, 11th, #5 and major 7th intervals. It shares no common notes with G7. Instead, we have one extended and three altered tones. Yes, it produces a pretty tense sound! But this is useful if you're looking to achieve a brief outside-inside effect.

We've encountered the major 7th interval (Gb or F#) before and treated it as a passing note. Mostly we'll treat it the same here, though this first line allows it to work its dissonant magic for a whole 1/8th note!

Example 4u

The next line features a 1/16th note descending run in bar two, beginning on the #5, also known as the b13 (Eb) of G7. In the latter half of the bar the phrasing takes a punchy intervallic approach, which is mimicked over the Cmaj7 chord in bar three.

Example 4v

This substitute line begins on the 11th (C) of G7, the most inside sounding tone we have in the Ab7 arpeggio. The first four-note phrase also ends on C, before dropping down to the #5 (Eb) and ascending back to C.

Example 4w

The final Ab7 substitution example takes a Coltrane or Michael Brecker like approach to the phrasing, playing fast four-note clusters, and only plays the Gb note once, omitting it from the latter phrases.

Example 4x

4. Dominant 7 arpeggio a minor 3rd above the V chord

The final idea we'll look at is another minor 3rd shift idea. From the G7 chord, we'll shift up a minor 3rd to Bb7. Here's how the substitution sounds.

Example 4y

Example 4z

This is a very useful substitution because it contains two chord tones of G7, plus the b9 and #9 intervals. Here they are in order:

Bb7 = Bb (#9), D (5th), F (b7), Ab (b9).

Let's put the arpeggio to work in some melodic licks.

The first idea here takes the Coltrane approach to playing the substitution, using four-note clusters.

Example 4z1

Dm9   G7b9   Cmaj7

```
e|---------------------------------------------------------------------------|
B|-------------5-5-----------------------------------------------7-8-7--------7-10-7--|
G|-------7---------5-------7-7---------------6-4------6-----6-------------8---8-------|
D|-----7-5------------7---------7-------6-------6---6-9---7------------9-------------|
A|---5--------------------------8-6-8----------------------------------------------|
E|---------------------------------------------------------------------------------|
```

Here's a more challenging idea with a mostly continuous stream of 1/16th notes. Give the lick a slow run through to begin with and work out an economical fingering that you're comfortable with.

Example 4z2

Dm9   G7b9   Cmaj7

```
e|----------------------------------------------------------------------------------|
B|-----10-13-10--------------------------6-9-6------6-9---10----12-13-10-------------|
G|---10----------10----------------7---7-------7---------------------------9-12-11-10|
D|-12----------------12-10---------6-8----------8-6-8-6-----------------------------|
A|-----------------------12-10-0-10-7---5-8----------------------------------------|
E|--------------------------------------------------------------------------------|
```

Next, a swinging example that omits the Bb note from the substitute line and emphasizes the Ab (b9) of G7.

Example 4z3

Dm9   G7b9   Cmaj7

```
e|-------------------------------------------------------------------------------|
B|-----------------------------13-10-----------------------------------------------|
G|-----10-9-------------------13--------9------9-----7-------5---------4-----------|
D|---12-11-12---------------12---------10----9-----7-----5---------------------|
A|-----------12--------11------------------------------------------------------|
E|------------------------------------------------------------------3-----------|
```

Finally, here's a swinging line that arranges the substitution in an ascending triplet phrasing.

Example 4z4

Chapter Five: Combining Substitution Ideas

The power of arpeggio substitution truly reveals itself when we begin to play melodic ideas that *combine* arpeggios. Using more than one substitute for the dominant V chord means we can create licks that have more movement, and this gives us the scope to connect arpeggios all over the fretboard, moving towards a real mastery of the ii V I sequence.

In this chapter we'll combine arpeggios in two different ways:

- First by combining arpeggios of the same type e.g. all minor 9ths, or all major 7ths

- Second, by mixing and matching arpeggio types e.g. a minor 9 plus a major 7, or a minor 7 plus a dominant 7 etc.

First, let's look at some examples that combine arpeggios of the same type. Limited space won't allow us to explore an exhaustive list of every possible combination of arpeggios, so the examples included here have been chosen for a specific reason: they make for easy, memorable movements on guitar.

You'll notice that most are either whole step movements, half-step movements or minor third shifts. These are some of my favorite combinations, but the sky's the limit and you should experiment and explore new ideas and sounds during your practice times.

We'll begin by combining minor 9 arpeggios over the dominant V chord. One example lick is provided for each substitution to spark some ideas but take each concept and explore it thoroughly over the ii V I backing tracks.

Combined minor arpeggios

In the first example we combine two minor 9 substitutions a whole step apart, playing Dm9 them Em9 over the G7 chord.

One of the first and most obvious ways to apply this idea is simply to create a short melodic phrase and repeat it, transposed to the new arpeggio. Here we play a five-note melody using Dm9, then repeat it a whole step up to transpose it to Em9.

Example 5a

Now let's use the Dm9 substitution again, but this time pair it with Abm9, a half-step above the G7 chord. Let's try this with a more ambitious 1/16th note line. I recommend you play the whole thing slowly a few times to begin with, like an etude, to allow the sound of the substitution intervals to sink in.

Example 5b

```
Dm9                        G7♭9                          Cmaj7
T|------5--------|--5---8-5-------------5-4-7-4-|-----------------------8-10----|
A|--8-6-5--------|6-------6-5---5-6---4---------|-----------7-9-------------9---|
B|------------7--|--------------7------4--------|---------9---------------------|
 |                            6-4----|6--7-9-10-|
```

Next up is a minor 3rd shift idea. Here we begin with an Fm9 substitution for G7, then shift up a minor 3rd to Abm9.

Example 5c

```
Dm9                    G7♭9                                    Cmaj7
T|--------------|-------------------------------11----------|----------15-13----|
A|--------------|--------8-10---8---9-11-12--12-11----11-----|--12-12------------|
B|------7-5-----|--8-7-5----10----------------------------|
 |5-7-8----8-7-5|8-10-11-------|
```

Why not go to town on the minor 3rd shift idea and include *all four* possibilities before arriving back where we started?

In bar two, this line moves through Fm9, Abm9, Bm9 and Dm9 arpeggios.

It's a tricky line to play but is made easier once you realize that the same four-note structure is being used for each arpeggio, alternating between being played ascending and descending.

Once you have the shape of those four notes in mind, it's a case of executing a fourth or first finger slide to move smoothly between arpeggios. i.e. After the first four-note phrase, you'll slide your fourth finger from the 4th to 7th fret on the top string to play the next shape. Then you'll perform a first finger slide from the 4th to 7th fret on the second string to get into position for the third arpeggio, etc.

Example 5d

Combined major arpeggios

Next we combine major 7 arpeggios. Back in Chapter Two we substituted a major 7 chord a half-step above the ii chord (Ebmaj7 over G7). Here, that substitution is used and paired with Fmaj7, a whole step movement.

Example 5e

We can enrich a major 7 arpeggio by adding the 9th. The following line combines Fmaj9 and Abmaj9 substitute arpeggios in bar two, which results in a minor 3rd shifting motif.

Example 5f

This idea combines Dbmaj7 and Abmaj9 arpeggio substitutes over G7 and uses shapes that enables the line to be played in one zone of the neck.

Example 5g

Combined minor 7b5 arpeggios

Next we will combine a series of minor 7b5 arpeggios. We begin by putting together Bm7b5 and Am7b5 arpeggios, a whole step apart, to form an undulating line.

Example 5h

The next line uses Bm7b5 again, this time preceded by a Dm7b5 arpeggio. The Dm7b5 part of the line uses a *shape one* arrangement, launched from the fifth string root note. The Bm7b5 part uses notes that fall in the same zone of the neck, so we can ascend the first arpeggio and descend the second.

Example 5i

For the next example, let's put together two arpeggios located a half-step apart: Em7b5 and Fm7b5. We saw in Chapter Three that Em7b5 contains two chord tones of G7 (root, 5th), an extended note (13th), and one altered note (#9). Fm7b5 also contains two G7 chord tones (3rd, b7), and two altered tones (#5, b9).

Put the two arpeggios together and we can spell out the full sound of G7, plus add one extended and three tension notes. It's a powerful combination to experiment with.

Let's take a moment to analyze the effect of the line in Example 5j.

The first five notes spell out the Em7b5 arpeggio. Over G7 it creates the following sound: 13th, root, #9, 5th and 13th repeated. This shape is moved up one fret and repeated, note for note to spell Fm7b5. This time, it creates the sound of the b7, b9, 3rd, #5 and a repeat of the b7.

For the last four notes of bar two we switch back to Em7b5, where we spell out the root, #9, 5th and root again of G7.

Example 5j

Combined Minor and Major arpeggios

A logical next step is to begin combining arpeggios of different chord qualities, mixing and matching them to taste. There are numerous possible permutations of this idea, but the next few examples take a first step in this direction by combining minor 7/minor 9 arpeggios with major 7s.

Example 5k combines Em7 and Fmaj9 arpeggios over the G7 chord. Both of these arpeggios contain the G root note, so if we want to give our altered line a more grounded sound, we can launch the first arpeggio from its G note.

Example 5k

Next we're going to pair Fm9 and Abmaj7 to play a substitute line over G7. Analyze these arpeggios and you'll see that they contain nearly all the same notes:

Fm9 = F, Ab, C, Eb, G

Abmaj7 = Ab, C, Eb, G

Fm9 has all the notes of Abmaj7 plus its F root.

So, why not just play Fm9 then?

This is a good reminder of why we've been exploring substitution ideas through multiple chord forms. As guitar players we are creatures of habit. Say "Fm9" to us and we'll immediately think of certain shapes on the fretboard where we can access that sound. Say "Abmaj7" and we'll think of a different set of shapes – because we do instinctively tend to think *shapes* rather than *notes*.

So, the act of combining two different but related shapes results in an important goal for us as improvisers: it opens up many more melodic options on the fretboard that we can easily jump into, using knowledge that we already possess.

Here's how this combination sounds. In bar two, we ascend the Fm9 arpeggio from its root note on the fourth string, 3rd fret, then descend a familiar Abmaj7 chord shape, ascending back up to transition into bar three.

Example 5l

Dm9   G7b9   Cmaj7

In the next example we combine minor and major arpeggios whose roots are located a whole step apart: Fm9 paired with Ebmaj7. As in the previous example, we ascend the minor 9 arpeggio and descend the major 7.

Example 5m

Dm9   G7b9   Cmaj7

Combined substitute ii V movements

Here's another way in which we can create some unique substitution ideas. In previous chapters we explored the sound of both minor and dominant substitutions, and in the next set of examples we combine these sounds to create a substitute "ii V" movement over the G7 chord.

The first example combines Fm7 and Bb7 arpeggios. Before you play this line, just play the chord sequence:

| Dm7 G7 | Fm7 Bb7 | Cmaj7 |

You'll probably recognize this sound from the comping of Joe Pass, Martin Taylor and other players. Instead of playing a bar each of Dm7 – G7 – Cmaj7, the idea here is to play a "quick ii V" i.e. to compress the Dm7 to G7 change into one bar, then in bar two play a substitute ii V (in this case Fm7 to Bb7) before returning to the harmony in bar three.

We are representing this comping idea in arpeggio form, played over the original chord changes.

Here the arpeggios are played with the note order sequenced to create smooth transitions between chords.

Example 5n

The remaining two ideas in this chapter are also examples of "quick ii V" substitutions. Play through each one with chords before you play the line.

| Dm7 G7 | Abm7 Db7 | Cmaj7 |

Abm7 and Db7 share the notes Ab and B, which means we can play the arpeggios in the same region of the neck and focus our line on their note differences.

Example 5o

Finally, a combination of Ebm7 and Ab7 arpeggios.

| Dm7 G7 | Ebm7 Ab7 | Cmaj7 |

Example 5p

We've only scratched the surface of what's possible in this chapter. There are a vast number of combinations we could put together to create new melodic ideas. Explore these ideas in your practice times and private study. In the final chapter we're going to workshop a jazz standard and look at how to apply substitution ideas to modernize a well-known tune.

Chapter Six: Applying Substitution Ideas to a Jazz Standard

In this final chapter, we're going to apply a selection of the ideas we've looked at to a jazz standard. Again, space prohibits us from exploring every option – that can be for your own practice sessions as you jam over the backing tracks – but I'll show you how to begin mixing and matching ideas to create movement and melodic interest. This is a principle you can apply to any jazz standard you want to breathe fresh life into.

We're all familiar with the chord changes of the evergreen standard *Autumn Leaves* and this tune, which contains both a major and minor ii V I within its first eight bars, is the ideal canvas on which to test our substitution ideas.

We're playing it in the key of G Major / E Minor. Let's begin with the first four bars:

| Am7 | D7 | Gmaj7 | Cmaj7 |

Drawing from previous chapters, we'll pick a selection of substitutions for the V chord (D7) in this sequence and compose a melodic line for each one.

Variations

To get us started, here are a few possible approaches that all use minor 9 arpeggio substitutions found in Chapter One. Each variation is demonstrated with one lick.

The first variation is to substitute a minor 9 chord a half-step above the root of the V chord, in this case: D7 = Ebm9.

At the end of bar two, notice how the F and Gb notes of Ebm9 target the root note of the Gmaj7 chord and sound like a typical bebop line with chromatic approach notes.

Example 6a

Variation two uses the minor 9 substitution a minor 3rd above the ii chord: Am7 = Cm9. In bar two, the notes of Cm9 are organized into Michael Brecker style four-note cells, and descend the neck in a 1/16th note run.

Example 6b

Variation three uses the minor 9 chord a b5 above the V chord: D7 = Abm9

In bar two of this idea, we play a doubling-back idea, climbing Abm9 arpeggio notes on the first string before transitioning into a descending run.

Example 6c

Next, we're going to use each of these three variations again, but this time in the context of the minor ii V i section of the chord changes. In other words, we'll apply the *same substitution principles* to the new chord changes.

Bars 5-8 of the *Autumn Leaves* changes are played as follows:

| F#m7b5 | B7 | Em7 | % |

Our first variation was to substitute a minor 9 chord a half-step above the root of the V chord. In this sequence, B7 is the V chord, so the minor 9 a half-step above it is Cm9.

"Hang on, I've just played Cm9 on the first four bars," you may be thinking!

Of course, you're right. During the Major ii V I section of the tune, Cm9 substituted for Am7. Now we're using it as a substitute for B7. So, if you wanted, Cm9 could be your go-to substitution for the whole tune. The more you dig into this subject, the more you'll come to realize the interchangeability of these ideas.

Let's hear how the Cm9 substitution sounds in this setting.

Example 6d

Let's continue the process and repeat the concept of substituting a minor 9 arpeggio a minor 3rd above the ii chord. This yields Am9 as the substitute arpeggio (F# to A equals a minor 3rd interval).

Example 6e

The third variation we used was the minor 9 arpeggio a b5 above the V chord. In this instance, B7 = Fm9.

Example 6f

It's time to pause for breath and take a brief review.

We've used just *one* arpeggio type and *three* substitution concepts, and this has already opened up a vast array of sonic possibilities for soloing. Now let's combine some of these ideas and play longer melodic lines over the complete eight-bar A section.

You can pick and choose from the above substitutions as you desire, but here's something to get you started. This example brings together two minor 9 variations. We can therefore view the progression like this, with the substitutes indicated in square brackets:

| Am7 | [Ebm9] | Gmaj7 | Cmaj7 |

| F#m7b5 | [Fm9] | Em7 | % |

To engage with this idea, first of all play through the progression very slowly, spelling out the sound of the chords with simple arpeggios. Refer back to the arpeggio shapes of Chapter One if you need a refresher. Allow your ears to adjust to the sound of the substitutions and visualize where you could move on the fretboard to connect the arpeggios with melodic lines.

After you've spent some time acclimatizing, play through the following short solo.

Example 6g

Let's try a different combination of substitutions. This time we'll combine both b5 substitution options, so that we now view the progression like this:

| Am7 | [Abm9] | Gmaj7 | Cmaj7 |

| F#m7b5 | [Fm9] | Em7 | % |

As before, take some time to play through the progression slowly, outlining each chord very simply. Once you've fixed the sound in your ears, try this extended melodic line.

Example 6h

We could continue swapping and changing these minor 9 variations to create more melodic ideas, but instead let's move on and repeat the exercise with two major 7 arpeggio substitutions.

The first variation, for the Major ii V I part of the progression, is to play a major 7 arpeggio a half-step above the V chord:

D7 = Ebmaj7.

The second variation, for the Minor ii V i part, is to play a major 7 arpeggio a b5 above the V chord:

B7 = Fmaj7.

Let's combine these variations over the eight-bar A section.

We can now view the progression like this (substitutions in square brackets):

| Am7 | [Ebmaj7] | Gmaj7 | Cmaj7 |

| F#m7b5 | [Fmaj7] | Em7 | % |

Here's how the new substitutions sound in an extended line.

Example 6i

We're just scratching the surface here. We've used two arpeggio types and a handful of variations. We could go on to use minor 7b5 and dominant 7 arpeggios, then apply *all* the substitution ideas for each arpeggio type, creating a virtually limitless supply of melodic material.

We can't work through all the options here, but below are a few different takes on the A section chords using substitutions you learned in earlier chapters.

Rather than spell out all the substitutions for you, this time do your own analysis of the concepts in use. I'll show the substitute arpeggios in square brackets as before – you just need to work out the interval relationships between the V chord and the substitution.

Before we get started, to reset our brains, here's a reminder of the original chord changes!

| Am7 | D7 | Gmaj7 | Cmaj7 |

| F#m7b5 | B7 | Em7 | % |

Below is a solo based on the full A section of the tune. It's a more challenging piece, with some fast arpeggiation in the style of Jonathan Kreisberg. Here are the substitute arpeggios being used:

| Am7 | [Ab7] | Gmaj7 | Cmaj7 |

| F#m7b5 | [Cm9 Abm9] | Em7 | % |

| Am7 | [Am7b5] | Gmaj7 | Cmaj7 |

| F#m7b5 | [Cmaj7] | Em7 | % |

The B section chords of *Autumn Leaves* are essentially contained in the A section, so you already have melodic ideas to play over the whole tune.

Example 6j

When it comes to applying these substitution ideas, I'm sure you can see that the melodic possibilities are almost inexhaustible, not to mention potentially mind boggling. That's the reason I chose to limit the number of substitutions used in this chapter – yet that still resulted in a vast array of musical options.

With this in mind, to conclude I want to give you a practice method by which you can begin to introduce these ideas into your playing in a practical way that won't fry your brain.

Practice Method

- First, pick a workhorse tune like *Autumn Leaves* or another favorite standard. Ideally, one that has both major and minor ii V Is within the progression

- Pick *one* minor 9 arpeggio substitution that you like the sound of

- Use *only* this substitution and solo over the tune, using it to replace the V chord for *both* the major and minor ii V I sequences

- Get to know the sound of this arpeggio thoroughly and learn the arpeggio shapes you need to play over the tune

- *Play, play, play* until that substitution begins to fall easily under the fingers and you can hear it even before you play it

- Now pick another standard in a different key and repeat the process, still using the same substitution

That's the whole method. Next, revisit the tunes you selected and repeat the process using just one *major 7* substitution idea.

- Go through the process from beginning to end, using *only* that substitution the entire tune.

- Once you have become fluent with the second arpeggio, combine it with the first.

- Use the minor 9 arpeggio for the first half of the tune and the major 7 for the second half. Then, swap them around. Work with them until you can play them fluently and interchangeably.

- Next, pick a minor 7b5 or dominant 7 arpeggio substitution and start the process again.

- This is a reliable way of incorporating these sounds into your playing in a practical, memorable manner that is not too overwhelming.

There is a lot of woodshedding ahead, for sure, but this approach will pay long term dividends in your playing. It will keep you creative and is a way of constantly stimulating new melodic ideas, so that you're always discovering something new to play. It's a great way to keep your playing sounding fresh and avoid the clichés.

Have fun with it, and if you find a substitution you really love on a specific tune, post a video of you playing it in the **FundamentalChangesInGuitar** Facebook group or tag us on Instagram for a share.